THE PREACHER'S THEME TO-DAY

The Preacher's Theme To-Day

Four Lectures
Delivered at the College of Preachers, Washington

BY

WILLIAM TEMPLE

Archbishop of York

LONDON
SOCIETY FOR PROMOTING
CHRISTIAN KNOWLEDGE
NORTHUMBERLAND AVENUE, W.C. 2
1936

Published in the United States of America by
The Morehouse Publishing Company, under
the title " The Centrality of Christ."

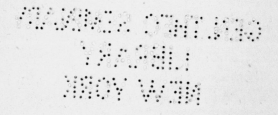

MADE IN GREAT BRITAIN

INTRODUCTORY NOTE

THESE four lectures were delivered at the College of Preachers at Washington, an institution of which I greatly wish that we had the like in the Church of England. They formed the subject of discussion with the group of clergymen—mainly young—who were gathered there, and were framed partly to supply points for such discussion. They are not to be regarded as a complete statement, even in outline, of the subjects handled.

I must express here my deep gratitude to the warden of the College, Bishop Rhinelander, for all the kindness which surrounded me during the conference. It made a rather arduous week entirely delightful.

WILLIAM EBOR:

December 20, 1935.

CONTENTS

CHAP.   PAGE

      INTRODUCTORY NOTE V

  I. REVELATION I

  II. THE INCARNATION 25

  III. SIN AND ATONEMENT 45

  IV. CHRISTIANITY, ETHICS, AND POLITICS . . 63

CHAPTER I

REVELATION

OUR subject in this lecture is " Revelation." In my own mind I am quite convinced that this is the centre of the most important of all theological problems of our time. A generation or so ago there was still active in the world a philosophy which held that all conduct and all that is described as spiritual could be accounted for in the terms of the physical sciences. Materialism, as it was known at the end of the nineteenth century and at the beginning of the twentieth, took that shape. And it was undoubtedly a very great gain for the presentation of the Christian faith when, alike in scientific and in philosophical circles, materialism came to be generally discounted.

Its place has been taken, first, by a philosophy which uses spiritual language and aims at preserving what it has become our custom to call spiritual values, but which has been disposed to take over from the old kind of materialism a sense of reality as a closed system in which every part depends upon every other part in the scheme of the whole, so that the principle of reality itself, the ultimate power, whether called God or not, is thought of as guiding all events but truly revealing Himself in no one event. He is regarded as doing everything in general, but not as doing anything in particular. It is a position not very far removed from the higher versions of Indian philosophy for which the ultimate principle is apparent in completeness in everything that exists or occurs.

So, when we think of the chief tendencies of our time, we can safely leave out of account the old-fashioned materialism, or what is now called Mechanical Determinism. I do not think there is now, at any rate in Europe, any very considerable school of thought which seriously believes that the methods and categories of the physical sciences can account for anything like the whole range of human experience. But there is in place of that, first of all, the philosophy associated with Russian Communism, Dialectical Materialism. This insists strongly, as I understand it, upon the distinction between matter and mind. Each acts according to its own laws, and the laws are different; it is not possible to account for mind in terms of the physical sciences, but only in the terms of the science appropriate to it. And these two are in perpetual interaction, so that there is no event, at any rate in human history, for which you can account in purely physical terms.

None the less, mind is regarded, first of all, as active only in response to a material situation presented to it, so that priority, so to speak, always lies with the material. And, secondly and far more important, the mental sciences are conceived on the strict analogy of the physical sciences, and though the laws of psychology may be quite different from the laws of physics, they are yet of the same kind in that they seek to account for all events in the terms of cause and effect.

As against such a philosophy, the distinction which it is vitally important to draw is that between causes and reasons. The cause of our conduct will generally contain a great deal more than the reasons which we should advance in justification of it. There is our whole personal history and the way in which we were treated as children. We have been given dispositions in certain directions, partly by inherited nature, partly by the influence of our home and other training brought to bear upon that nature. And all of this inclines us rather in one direction or another in face of the various kinds of circumstance that meet us.

But no one who is asked why he has actually done some unusual thing accounts for it by giving his personal history or referring to the temperamental peculiarities of his nurse. He will discuss what it was that the situation seemed to him to require and what good result he hoped to obtain by means of his action. In other words, when he tries to account for what he has done, it will not be in terms of causes acting from the past upon the present and through that to the future, but in terms of the future and of conduct in the present such as to secure a desirable future result. He is acting by reasons, and not only by causes.

Of course it is true that all of us act very largely under the influence of causes, physical and psychological. But we are none of us content to regard that as the whole account of our action, and there are very few, even of the most materialistic psychologists, who are prepared to accept this account of their own psychology. If a psychologist assures me that I believe in God because of the way in which my nurse used to treat me, I must retort that he only holds that belief concerning my belief because of the way in which his nurse used to treat him. It is a game that any of us can play quite indefinitely, the fact being that psychology has a great deal to teach us about the way in which we tend to form our opinions, and about the way in which we may make real and vital to ourselves convictions which we hold on intellectual grounds alone; but it cannot, of itself, pronounce one way or the other upon the truth or falsehood of those convictions.

The first claim, then, that we have to make, is that there exist in the world beings, namely ourselves, of such a kind as to act by reasons and not only by causes; or, if you like to put it that way, not only under the influence of compelling forces, but under the influence of what seems to us good. And for that conception, so far as I know, materialism, whether mechanical or dialectical, makes no allowance whatever.

I believe it is true that Dialectical Materialism must, in the long run, develop into some form of

Theism or Pantheism through its own inherent dialectic; for I believe that once the distinction between mind and matter is allowed, attention to the behaviour of mind is bound to bring men to an interpretation of experience in spiritual terms. We have to face the fact that in the world of our time this has not, at present, occurred with those who adopt this position, and we are face to face with a great organized mass of human thought resting upon a position which, though different from the old-fashioned materialism, is identical with it at the relevant point.

I do not say more about that fact because our quarrel with that philosophy is fundamental and complete. The denial of freedom to man, at least in the sense of allowing that his action is determined by what he thinks good and not only by causes operating upon him from the past, is quite vital to our whole position. We must insist upon that with those who deny it. We are in complete diametrical disagreement. I do not believe, in fact, that anybody in practice can hold that sort of materialist position. To use an illustration I have used before, everybody does, in fact, distinguish sharply between jumping into a river for a swim and being pushed into a river either by accident or through the malice of some passer-by. Nobody supposes that these two are the least alike, and the difference is quite clearly shown in their emotional reactions on the two events. In the former case the man is likely to exclaim, no doubt mendaciously, that it's delicious; but in the latter he speaks with a deeper sincerity of what he feels concerning the man who pushed him in.

With Dialectical Materialism we have merely a direct quarrel. We go back to that other view that has been more prevalent, at any rate in my own country, and I think probably also here, which has escaped from materialism altogether in the sense that it does recognize the category of good, or value, as a really determining influence in conduct, but which interprets the ultimate principle of reality as something merely exhibiting itself in all grades of reality and nowhere taking definite action. That, I wish to suggest as the distinguishing mark between Theism and Pantheism. Does God take definite and specific action, or is He only in a general sense the source of all that is or happens?

Now, let us recognize at once that the best Pantheism is very close to Theism. Some who hold this position, from which I think we have to distinguish our own as Christians, are able to employ very Christian language, but there is, none the less, an angle of divergence, and the divergent lines reach to the Antipodes. We are familiar with the principle of the watershed, where two springs may lie very close together, but the water that comes from those springs flows out into oceans far apart. The Rhine and the Rhone rise in the Swiss Alps very close together, but one flows into the North Sea and the other into the Mediterranean. When you are at the heights, you may say it makes very little difference which stream you have struck, but as you follow the valleys down, you come to very different places.

So it is with this distinction between Theism as we have received it through the tradition of the Bible and the Pantheism which is more definitely the product of a philosophy based upon that of the ancient Greeks. It is a very tempting kind of philosophy; it gives us a conception of the eternal as the ground of the temporal which is intellectually satisfying, more easily, I think, than we can reach that along the other road. Moreover, the life of the intellect is, within itself, bound to be directed mainly towards the acquirement of knowledge and understanding, and for purposes of understanding, what we most desire is always to arrive at some fixed principle which governs all process of change.

If, then, we are able to arrive at some principle capable of accounting for the existence of the universe and all things in it, that seems to satisfy the intellectual demand. And so long as we do not bring into our data and put into a prominent place among them the requirement of the moral nature of mankind, we are likely to be content with this view.

Dr. Edwyn Bevan is always insisting, I think quite rightly, that the great distinction among men is not between Eastern and Western, but between those who have come strongly under the influence of the Bible and those who have not. He points out that the civilization of ancient Greece, right down to the time of the Gospel story, bears a very close resemblance to the situation in India to-day. There is in each a lofty philosophy, often astonishingly alike in the spirituality of their ultimate conceptions; and there is a profound degradation of human life in other parts of society; and the former is not only incapable of effecting any improvement in the latter, but does not feel under any constraining impulse to do so. Those for whom conduct is, in Matthew Arnold's phrase, nine-tenths of life, have learned that principle from the Bible. It has come from the conviction that God is not to be conceived as a static perfection, whose nature appears in all things that are grounded in that perfection, but is to be conceived as living and righteous will, so that we come closest to Him not when, with our mind, we obtain a wide conspectus of truth, but when in our purposes we are united with His righteous purpose.

And, while there have been great moral prophets outside the biblical tradition, conspicuously Zoroaster, their influence has never been permanent. It is only in the Bible and what has sprung from the Bible that we have a continuous tradition of belief in moral conduct as the central concern of human life, and we have that because from the Bible we have learned the faith in God as righteous will. We shall have to come back to that distinction again, when we are considering the question of the importance of the historical event of the Incarnation.

I think that the great movement on the continent of Europe associated with the name of Karl Barth is very largely, though not entirely, to be understood as a violent reaction towards this biblical sense of God as righteous will over against the strongly immanental tendencies which have been characteristic of German theology in the last period. The doctrine of the personality of God is, as I think, fundamental to the biblical religion, whether in the Old or in the New Testament, and it is incompatible with any doctrine of God conceived as purely or even as mainly immanent.

Immanence is a truth as far as it goes. The whole Pantheistic scheme of which I have been preaching is a truth so far as it goes; but at the vital point it fails because it does not supply the necessary ground for giving supremacy to the moral element in life.

German theology had gone very far in the direction of conceiving God as an immanent spirit—if that is an appropriate word for what is purely immanent, for I would rather say principle— guiding men forward to a fuller and richer life, finding its fullest expression in our Lord, who is, none the less, in such theology regarded as first and foremost a human being in whom there is very conspicuous manifestation of this divine principle.

Over against such a view Karl Barth and his

B

school have insisted that God is always to be conceived as the living God who strikes into human
history where and as He will, whose action is not
to be thought of as in any way conditioned by the
process of that history, but simply and solely by
the operation of His own will. Personally, I think
that, as in most reactions, there is here a very
great one-sidedness, and therefore also exaggera-
tion, for not only does Barth maintain that we
learn through revelation what could never have
been reached by a philosophy of experience, but
also that it is quite impossible to take that revelation and, by its help, to construct a philosophy of
experience. And there are certain questions which,
as it seems to me, a thorough-going disciple of
Karl Barth must find it very hard to answer.

Thus, for example, supposing that he meets a
Moslem who should say to him, " All that you
have to tell us about the Word of God is magnificent and true. You only make one mistake.
You take it to be in the Bible; whereas, in fact,
it is in the Koran." What is Barth to answer on
his own premise? The only disciple of his whom
I have asked said that he could not answer at all.

That is not necessarily an objection to a prophet.
When Jeremiah was confronted with those who
claimed also to be prophets of the Lord and said
the exact opposite of what he was saying, he had
no effective reply except to say that it wasn't true;
that if they said that, they had not stood in the
counsel of the Most High; and the audience must

be left to judge. It is not the prophet's business to argue, but to proclaim. But it is the business of the theologian to make at least some progress in the direction of rendering intelligible that truth which the prophet has delivered, and here it seems to me that the Barthian theology must always fail.

Or, again, I should wish to ask, if God is " wholly other," and that is all that really can be said about Him apart from the specific oracles in which His will is declared, how is it that we can even understand that concerning Him? How are we able to receive these oracles? If the fall of man has carried us so far away that there is left in us no effective trace of the divine image in which we were made, by what power do we recognize the revelation when it comes? And once again I do not know what is the Barthian answer. That may be due to deficient study of the Barthian writings, but I find it hard to conceive what the answer should be.

None the less, I think we owe, all of us, a profound debt of gratitude to this school of theology which has brought again into the forefront (though I think that it has given it too much isolation) what is the fundamental principle of the biblical revelation—that God is righteous will, that He has a purpose, that our duty is to conform to that purpose, that it is possible for us to depart from that purpose, and that such departure is sin.

Or, we may put it in the elementary phrase adopted by Lord Balfour in the first series of his

Gifford Lectures, to which I think altogether too little attention has been given, on Theism and Humanism—the question whether or not we believe that God " takes sides." Is He only the universal immanent principle, or does He take sides? Is there any sense in language such as that about coming to the help of the Lord against the mighty? Does that represent anything in the real constitution of the world?

And all of this reaches its climax in the question which is our question here: Are there specific acts of revelation? Is it our duty, as we try to form our conception of God, to take as wide a basis of experience as possible and, from that, by an inductive process, construct a conception of God which shall do justice to the facts in the scientific fashion? Or are there acts recorded in which God has Himself taken the necessary steps to declare His own nature to our mind?

Now let us begin by recognizing the truth in the position that we do not adopt—and may I in parenthesis say that that is the only fruitful method of controversy? It is to be noticed that no one ever persuades another person by what is called a fighting speech. When somebody makes a " magnificent fighting speech " his supporters cheer and his opponents are unmoved. You can never persuade anybody of anything unless you first recognize the truth in the position which he holds and admit it, or, indeed, if possible, strongly assert it. That being done, the opponent, realizing

that you understand his case, may be ready also
to listen to what more, also, you have to say.
But if you begin by merely saying that he is wrong,
he will reply by saying that you are wrong, and
the ordinary political dog fight ensues. Let us at
least avoid that in connection with religion!

It is true that if there is any revelation at all,
then everything whatsoever must be revelation,
because the Being who is to be revealed is the
God of heaven and earth, the Maker of all things,
and the character of the Maker must appear to
some extent in what He makes. And therefore in
all things that exist at all there must be some
trace of Him. Though it may be very little of
His nature that He has shown in any one thing,
yet there must be some trace of the character of
the author of its being. Unless all things are
revelation in this degree, nothing can be revelation
at all. Either God is not the God of all the earth,
and then He is not God, or else the God who
gives the revelation is also He who, as Creator,
has originated all other things.

No doubt there are many facts which, if we isolate
them and attend to them alone without their context, would give us no true conception of God at
all; but then such things are not really " facts."
The " fact " is whatever has occurred in its whole
setting, both past and future, and therefore it is
always true that so long as our knowledge is limited
at all we have not complete and final knowledge
of anything.

All our knowledge of the world is defective in that there are some parts of the universe, related in the whole scheme of causation to what we are studying, of which we are still ignorant. The degree of that limitation, of course, varies very vastly, and it may be that for all practical purposes the consequent defect in knowledge can be ignored; but for theoretical purposes it is important. Thus we may isolate some horrible occurrence and fail to find in it any trace of divine character at all. The claim of anyone who says that all things in some degree reveal God, must be that if only we could see it in its whole context there would be perceptible in the movement, of which this fact is an episode, at least some trace of the divine character and will. Unless all things are revelation, nothing can be revelation. Unless the rising of the sun reveals God, the rising of the Son of Man from the dead cannot reveal God.

Then, supposing that God is conceived in terms of personality and will, and we are in the least degree thorough-going with that analogy, it will follow at once that some of those events which we are now regarding as His action will represent Him much more fully than others.

We are all familiar with the fact that nine-tenths of the actions of the greatest of men are indistinguishable from those of average mankind. He gets up in the morning in much the same way and puts on the same kind of clothes and eats the same kind of breakfast, and if we are really going to tabulate all the things he does all day, nine-tenths will be exactly like what everybody else is doing, and there will be nothing to show that he is a great man at all.

The late Dean of Norwich, Dr. Beeching, used to delight in the story of the old campaigner who said, " Now I will show you how the great Duke of Wellington used to eat figs "; but it turned out to be the old method—quadrisection down the stalk, and then four licks. Nobody understands the Duke of Wellington the least better for knowing that he ate figs like an ordinary human being. But you do understand him better if you know that on the way out to the Peninsular War his aide-de-camp came to the cabin of his ship and said the captain was convinced that the ship would not live, and was expected to sink within fifteen minutes. " In that case," said Sir Arthur, " I shall not take off my boots."

It is always true that what gives occasion for the distinctions of personality to reveal themselves is something in the nature of an emergency, not the carrying on of the ordinary routine of life, such as the sun rising and the sun setting in the life of the universe, but an occasion which, in greater or less degree, constitutes an emergency to which people react in very different ways; and sometimes it is only in the face of a very great crisis that the real character of a personality appears.

There may have been two men living side by

side of whom, on the whole, one seemed to show more energy and decisiveness of character than the other, though with no very great degree of difference between them. But a great crisis comes, and this one who has hitherto been taken to be the stronger personality gives way before it, while the other, perhaps because of the very reserve that he has practised till that moment, rises to it and masters it, and only then do men know what it was that was in him all the time. The natural expression that we use at such a time is, " I did not know he had it in him." We then recognize what always had been there but had never been revealed.

I cannot see how, in any scheme of things, the extension of the principle of personality to the explanation of the universe can avoid that analogy. For the most part we must expect to find that the divine action proceeds by a perfectly regular process. It will only be set aside when there is sufficient occasion. Only, if we are approaching the matter this way, let us be quite clear that the regular process is just as much a divine action as is the departure from that regularity when occasion demands it. It is not that there is a fixed natural order laid down once for all by God, and since left alone, with which from time to time He interferes; it is that all the while He is acting, only all the while it is appropriate, on most occasions, to follow a regular course, as does the ordinary man of regular habit in the conduct of his daily life.·

But, where some sufficient emergency occurs, this course can be set aside, because all the while it is grounded not in physical necessity, but in the divine will, or, to use the language we were using earlier in this lecture, in the divine apprehension of what is good. Now, if anything will call forth specially revealing acts of God, if He is a God of righteousness, it must be the fact of sin. If God is rightly thought of as first and foremost righteous, however much that conception of righteousness is to be deepened into the Christian idea of love, then certainly it must be true that the event or fact which may call Him forth from routine activities, so to speak, will be what is diametrically opposed to this which is His own nature. It will be sin which gives the chief occasion for the divine revelation, and that, of course, is what the Bible presents to us. It presents to us a condition of mankind as departed from the way of God, and while God's care for man would be constant whether he had sinned or no, it is the fact of his sin which makes necessary the departures from the normal course of conduct.

It is in the Bible that Christians have found the record of the divine revelation, not alone but supremely. But being so much under the influence, in theology, of the tendencies due to Greek philosophy, they formed the idea that the content of revelation must be ideas capable of being formulated in propositions, and people began to speak very much about revealed truth. Consequently, as

Archdeacon Lilley has pointed out, it came as something of a scandal that the Bible contains so very little in the way of formulated ideas, or theological propositions, and such a very great deal else. I think that that divergence should set us inquiring again about what the Bible presents as the area in which the revelation is given, and, as I quote Archdeacon Lilley, I do not think he himself fully accomplishes the transition which he seems to think desirable, for he seems still to think that the *locus* of revelation, the place where supremely it occurs, is in the human mind. He escapes from the notion of a kind of dictated truth, but he leaves still the idea that what is of vital importance is something that happens within the mind.

Now, what goes on within the mind must be either intellectual formulation or imaginative apprehension. Broadly speaking, I think those cover the range of the mind's power of receiving any kind of truth. And as he is discarding the notion that revelation gives us intellectual truth in a formulated form, he leaves us with the idea that it rather comes in the poetic glow wherein the mind is wrapped into a union with the divine, and seeks to utter what it has experienced by those modes of expression which seem to force words to convey something beyond their ordinary meaning.

No doubt there is a great measure of truth, also, in that. But it has this great difficulty: that this kind of poetic apprehension is always very vague. It may stir deeply those who are in sufficient mental sympathy with the poet to enter into his experience as they read his utterances, but a good many people will be left untouched; and there is nothing definite there at all.

If that were so, we should have to accept the fact and make the best of it. But when you go to the Bible it does not seem to be so, for surely if we can put aside preconceptions for a moment and ask what it is in which the Bible is primarily interested, it is always in events. The Bible is, for the most part, a history book—a very peculiar kind of history book, no doubt, but a history book all the same. It is concerned, above all, with certain great cardinal events upon which the history of Israel turned: the events connected with the names of Abraham and Moses, the Exodus, Sennacherib, the Exile, and the Return.

It is perfectly true that the biblical writers have a different interest in these events from that which most historians have in the events that they narrate. The ordinary historian is always concerned with the questions, What were men aiming at? What did men accomplish? The biblical historian is always concerned with the question, What was the purpose of God? Or, what was the judgment of God?

We see it very clearly when we compare two events in the histories of Israel and England which are not entirely unlike. In each there is the record of a rebellion which was due to unpopular taxation. Solomon had gone in for magnificence.

When kings do that the people have to pay. So long as the magnificent king was there they were content. But the palace of Lebanon at Jerusalem bears much the same relation to the rebellion under Rehoboam as does the palace of Versailles to the French Revolution. When Rehoboam came to the throne, men came to him and asked that he make the burden lighter; and he declined; so they rebelled; and unless you read rather closely, you will not find out that what we call taxation had anything to do with it. It is just mentioned, but only just. It is mentioned when it is said that Rehoboam, after the conference, " sent out Adoram which was over the tribute and they stoned him with stones so that he died "; so Rehoboam knew the thing was serious. That is all there is about taxes.

Why? What should we think of an English historian who dealt with the reign of Charles I and who never mentioned benevolences, forced loans, and, above all, ship money? We should think he was writing history very badly. That is because the English historian would be concerned with the question, What was in the minds of men? The biblical historian is always concerned with the question, What was in the mind of God? But that to which he desires to relate the mind of God is always the event, and I want to suggest to you that on the biblical view the *locus*, the sphere, the area, of revelation, is primarily the historic event, not thoughts in men's minds at all, but the thing that happens—the deliverance from Egypt, the retreat of Sennacherib, the Exile, and the Return. In these things we are to read the action of God, His purpose, His judgment.

This can only be read, no doubt, under divine inspiration, but the prophet is primarily the man, not to whom God has communicated certain divine thoughts, but whose mind is illuminated by the divine spirit to interpret aright the divine acts; and the act is primary.

There is about an event this great quality: that it is in itself something quite definite. There may be different interpretations of it and approaches to it, but that is only because no one of the interpretations completely exhausts its significance. But it is in itself something not vague, but definite, to which we can all definitely relate ourselves. And that all comes to a climax in the subject which will be before us when we turn to consider the place of our Lord in Christian thought and experience; for there the primary fact is the Incarnation itself, that the Word was made flesh.

But it is also quite true that that fact would have been barren if there had not been those whose minds were illuminated to receive and understand it: "We beheld His glory." Both are necessary, but the central sphere of the revelation itself is in the event, not in the minds which apprehend it, though apart from them the revelation would not bear its fruit.

Then, once more, the subject-matter of this

revelation is, so far as I can see, twofold. It is God and the Church. I think Dr. Goudge is right when he maintains that there are, in the end, only two doctrines in the Bible: the doctrine of God and the doctrine of the Church. For the great concern of the Old Testament is with Israel, the divinely commissioned community. Under the influence of that subjectivist habit of mind about which we have already spoken, we have been disposed, in the last period, to treat the Old Testament as a series of human apprehensions of God, and there has lately been published in England, by a number of distinguished scholars, a series of handbooks for schools in which the one that deals with the Old Testament, so far as I can remember, never mentions Israel, and would accurately be described as what men at different dates thought about God.

But the interest of the Old Testament writers themselves is primarily with God and with Israel as the agent of His purpose. It is surely of great value to us, as we return to a perpetually fuller understanding of the social nature of man and realize how completely interdependent we are, that we should see how from the beginning God has been planning to act upon the world through a commissioned community which stretches back into the time when history merges into myth. If the name of Abraham stands rather for a tribal migration than for an individual, as some scholars tell us, that only underlines this point; for it

means that already there you have the community
conscious of its divine mission as history begins to
take definite shape. Here is the community
through which the righteous God will act. And
then those whose minds He illuminates to understand His dealings with that community come to
see how little adequate is the response which that
community is making. They become persuaded
that the divine purpose will be accomplished not
in Israel as a whole, but through a Remnant.
They come to see perpetually with greater clearness that Israel has received this truth concerning
the righteous God in order that it may pass that
truth on to all the world, " a light to lighten the
Gentiles." They look forward to the time when
the nations outside will be brought into this same
fellowship and when " Israel shall be the third
with Egypt and with Assyria " (the two great
enemies and menaces), " a blessing in the midst
of the earth, for the Lord of hosts hath blessed
them, saying "—and think how the conservatives
must have shuddered—" blessed be Egypt my
people, and Assyria, the work of my hands, and
Israel, my inheritance."

But then to the second Isaiah it becomes clear
that not even the Remnant will respond with
sufficient fulness. The servant of Jehovah is con-
tracted, so to speak, from the whole community to
the Remnant, and from the Remnant to a single
individual upon whom the Lord lays the iniquity
of us all. And so it happened; for when the

Messiah came, though there were a few who recognized Him, their faith was not stable; even the Rock-man was one of those who forsook Him and fled, and when, a little later, he followed afar off, it was to the place where he would stand and warm himself, and say, " I do not know the man."

In the supreme moment of the whole world's history the true Israel was concentrated in the person of the Messiah alone as He bore the iniquity of us all. In Him that Israel of God was reconstituted, freed now from all national limitations, to go forth as the Christian Church, carrying the Gospel of what the Messiah had accomplished and of the love of God made known in Him, to bring all nations into the allegiance of the God thus revealed.

The redeemed community becomes the great theme of the New Testament, apart from the record of the Messianic acts of Christ. And in that community we still are members, not by any racial inheritance nor by any choice of our own wills, but by operation of the Holy Ghost.

CHAPTER II

THE INCARNATION

IN our consideration of the principle of revelation, it was suggested that the area or *locus* of the revelation is at least usually an objective event, but that for the right reading and interpretation of that event there is needed illumination of the Holy Spirit, so that actual and effective revelation takes place when there is a coincidence of the divinely guided event and the divinely illuminated mind, and for the fulness and effectiveness of revelation both factors are necessary.

That principle finds its fullest illustration in the Gospel story, for here the revelation is given in the fact of Christ. He is Himself the revelation. The event is primary: "The Word was made flesh." And yet it is also true that for this event to bring forth its spiritual fruit there must be hearts and minds sufficiently enlightened to appreciate the event for what it was: "We beheld His glory." If there had been none who could understand at all, then, though the Incarnation would have happened, and doubtless must have represented something in the eternal realm, yet, so far as we can tell, its effect upon this world and the satisfaction of our needs would have been entirely negative. While the event is primary, the perceiving mind is also necessary.

St. John sets before us the story of the Lord's life as a process of judgment wherein are distinguished those who can and those who cannot perceive what is before them. For " the Jews," as he always speaks of them, heard most of the words and saw most of the acts which the disciples also heard and saw, but they did not behold His glory. And the judgment works by sifting out men according to their capacity or incapacity to perceive what is before them. " This is the judgment, that light is come into the world and men chose darkness rather than light because their deeds were evil."

We begin, then, with the fact. And first it seems to me necessary to insist upon the vital importance of its historical occurrence. Why so? Let us contrast with the traditional doctrine of the Church the position set out in one of his letters by the great philosopher Spinoza, to whom the question had been put whether it was necessary to salvation to have knowledge of Jesus Christ; he answered that it is not necessary to salvation to know Christ according to the flesh, but that an entirely different view must be taken concerning that eternal Word which is the wisdom of God and has manifested itself in all things, and especially in the mind of man, and most of all, in Jesus Christ. According to such a doctrine, the vital matter is to know the wisdom of God. If you are able to know that without reference to the incarnate life of Christ, you have still obtained all that is necessary, and the Incarnation on such a view took place in order to make known that eternal wisdom.

It is revelation, and revelation only. Nothing is done by it, but something eternal is disclosed. And if that is true, then it might be held that it no longer matters whether the event is historical or mythical. For it could be held that it is still the true picture of what God eternally is, and the fact of its occurrence at a particular moment and in a particular place might be regarded as irrelevant.

There are very few who would call themselves Christians at all who take that view, but there are some who take a view that is to my mind not widely separated from it. They say that the Divine Spirit is manifest in all the world, which is true, and that He is supremely manifest in the character set before us in the Gospel, which is also true. Therefore, we have learned from this figure of the Gospel what is the character of God. We confess the divinity of Christ, but need not commit ourselves to His Deity. That is a distinction which, in England, has been emphasized rather strongly of late in some theological quarters, and one section of opinion calling itself orthodox and continuing to use the Nicene Creed to express itself is, in fact, in very close harmony with one section of Unitarian thought which accepts our

Lord as the supreme and sufficient manifestation
of divine character.

It seems to me that there are two fatal objections
to that view. The first is that it affords no ground
for answering the question how you are to be
assured in your belief that this figure discloses the
character of the eternal God. If something has
actually happened, then the ground for all reality
must, so to speak, be adequate to account for that
occurrence. But if it has been only dreamed, if
it is only a lofty conception framed in the imagina-
tion of pure souls, then, in face of what we know
of the actual world, how are we, with any security,
to cling to the belief that the ground of all reality
is better represented by such idealistic dreaming than
by the bitter experience of the grim side of life?

It is quite true that Christianity, by attaching
itself so closely to historical occurrences, is exposed
to critical attack on historical grounds in a way
which would not be true concerning a philosophy
that did not repose so definitely upon alleged facts,
but consisted rather in a necessary connection of
thought. Contingency is certainly admitted as
soon as the claim is made that the divine revelation
is offered in a particular historical occurrence.
But that introduction of contingency, with its
inevitable element of purely logical uncertainty,
is the price that has to be paid for a faith which
has its grip upon fact, because all fact is in that
sense contingent. It is never possible to prove
that what happened must have happened precisely

so and not otherwise. A knowledge of it always depends upon evidence, and the evidence is never in a logical sense absolutely cogent. We are always in the realm of probability, however high the probability may be. We do not, in connection with facts, ever reach that kind of certainty which belongs to a mathematical argument, and therefore, if our faith is to have a direct hold upon fact, it must be at least in contact with what is contingent, and it is hard to see how that can be unless it enters the contingent realm itself.

But there is more than this. If the life of Christ as recorded in the Gospels is only the dream of aspiring souls, then not only have we no ground for saying that God must be what is there set before us, but we have ground for saying that He is not. If God is indeed such love as is depicted in that story, then He must have taken upon Himself the sin and suffering of the world. And if there is no ground for supposing that He has actually done this, then the God who is supposed to be revealed is inferior to the image which is supposed to reveal Him. Christ is greater than God unless God Himself is in Christ actually and factually. St. John is perfectly justified in his insistence that that man is anti-Christ who denies that Jesus Christ came in the flesh. Not only must His coming be actual, but it must be actually He who comes. Both sides are indispensable. The event must have occurred upon the plane of history where other things happen.

All that is represented by the inclusion in the creed of the words "under Pontius Pilate" must be genuinely real, and He of whom these things are real must be Himself eternal God. Nothing else will give coherence, and the assurance which coherence brings, to the Christian conception both of God and of life.

Is such dogmatism a fetter to the human mind? In a period when men exalt liberty of mind as though it were almost the only sacred principle of life, is this dogmatism to be regarded as an enemy? There is much that might be said about this solitary exaltation of intellectual freedom, for after all the object of the mind should be its own subjugation to the truth. Its freedom must never be freedom to move according to its own impulses, but freedom to weigh the evidence in order that it may be subdued itself to the truth. The scientific inquirer is not allowed to pursue his own intellectual whims. His duty is to try to ascertain the facts, and to accept them even when they appear to be fatal to the theories which he has built up and on which perhaps he has also built his reputation. Intellectual humility is the necessary counterpart of intellectual freedom if that freedom is not to spell disaster. In the search of the mind, as everywhere else in human life, we are under authority—the authority of the truth. Consequently the question that we have to consider is whether, by all the tests that we can apply, this dogma exhibits the signs of truth. And if it does, then it is to be accepted, even though it should appear that many enticing lines of thought are for evermore shut out.

But there is a further point of great importance. While the dogma of the Incarnation is inevitably expressed in words, it is not the words that are themselves the object of faith. It points to a Person, and our allegiance is claimed only for that Person, and not for what is formulated concerning Him. The creeds are not objects of faith; they are expressions of a faith of which Christ is the object, and in regard to all such personal relationship there is scope for at least a great width of intellectual movement as we seek more and more perfectly to understand and to interpret the character with which we are confronted.

No one who has come to believe in a friend so as to feel sure that that friend would never betray him regards this assurance as a limit set to his intellectual freedom. It is quite true that he does exclude the possibility of speculation upon how he would behave if the friend betrayed that trust, but the exclusion of such lines of inquiry does not present itself as a fetter; and the dogma of the Incarnation will only seem to be intellectually a form of bondage if it is imposed upon people whose hearts are not yet in any way given to Christ.

Where there is personal experience of the redeeming power of Christ, no one will in fact find that the dogma concerning Him is intellectually restrictive. We cannot too often insist upon this point, that the centre of Christian faith is not an intellectual proposition, but a person, and the value of all the intellectual propositions and all the formulations of theology is that they give us guidance, resting upon the experience of multitudes of Christians, by which we may enter into that same relationship to Christ which those multitudes of Christians have already enjoyed. The moment that we separate the doctrine from the actual spiritual fellowship with Christ we begin to distort it, because the purpose of its existence is to be the guide to, as it is the interpretation of, this experienced fellowship, this communion with the Lord.

But again the objection is raised that in a world which has learned to think in categories of evolution and to believe in progress through the ages it is impossible to accept as final a revelation given two thousand years ago. Incidentally, it is always worth while to inquire how far the doctrine of evolution has anything to do with any reasonable notion of progress. At least in its biological form it seems to have very little connection with it. If you take an unarmed saint and confront him with a hungry tiger, there will be a struggle for existence culminating in the survival of the fittest, which means, of course, the fittest to survive in those conditions; but it will not be a survival of the ethically best. There is no reason to suppose that the struggle for existence always favours what is ethically admirable any more than there is any reason to suppose that a social order, if it may have the name, characterized by cut-throat competition, will always bring its best citizens to the top.

The idea of progress is rather different. No doubt in the nineteenth century men tended to imagine that progress goes on by itself. As Dean Inge has remarked, the War made that idea look rather silly, and the peace killed it outright. But while we may admit that progress is not something that happens automatically and has always to be achieved by deliberate effort, yet it does appear that if God has a purpose for mankind which is being worked out through the ages, we should expect to find that this fulfils itself by stages and that from stage to stage some real progress is discernible.

Nor is it possible to read history without perceiving that in many respects real progress is made, though not perhaps in the fundamental spiritual life. There is no reason, I think, to suppose that there are more people now making an earnest effort to conform to the will of God than there have been in previous generations. In fundamental spiritual direction of heart and soul there is, perhaps, no progress to be discerned. But there is progress to be discerned in the ordering of life which results from the efforts of these many generations in which some, at least, have been dedicating their faculties to the service of God and man. Their efforts have not been vain, and each generation starts from a point of vantage which those efforts have gained. And we have our own contribution to make in like manner. In such a sense, at least, progress seems, broadly speaking, to be a fact. How are we to relate that fact to a final revelation given two thousand years ago?

First, let us remember that in the Christian doctrine the divine activity of which the Incarnation is the focal point did not come to an end with the Ascension, and that there remained, and still remains, in the world the Body of Christ through which He is still active, carrying on the work which He then began. It is no part of Christian doctrine—indeed it is flatly contrary to Christian doctrine—to say that everything was then once and for all accomplished. Something of supreme importance was accomplished, but the application of that in every sphere of life has still to be worked out, and the Body of Christ as it has been hitherto and as we know it now is something which is in process of being built up into its fulness until we all come to constitute one perfect man, the measure of the stature of the completeness of the Messiah.

St. Paul certainly did not mean that each of us is to become a perfect man. The vision in his mind was that the "one man in Christ Jesus" who is constituted by members drawn from all the races of men is still growing to fulness of stature which will only be there when all men of all races have been grafted into the body and become its members. Plenty of room for as much progress as we can any of us hope to see is compatible with the finality of the revelation of the divine character in Jesus Christ.

Not only so; but the primary condition of making any progress is that the direction of movement should be fixed. Indeed, one of the great difficulties about making progress in social life is that our prophets change from generation to generation the direction in which they encourage us to walk. So soon as one panacea has been made the subject of thorough-going experiment, its defects are noticed and some correction in its constitution is supplied. Sometimes, indeed, the result of experimenting with a panacea is to awaken universal disgust and set people moving in precisely the opposite direction. But the primary requirement for making progress is that you shall go on and on in the same direction.

Certainly it will be a mistake to continue for ever in one direction if it is the wrong one, and we must be open to consider any new reflections that are offered us which may throw doubt upon the rightness of the direction in which we are moving. None the less, nothing can so much conduce to making progress as to have found the right direction and then pursue it without wavering. It is the claim of the Gospel that it gives us permanent direction for the conduct of our lives in Him who said, " I am the way, the truth, and the life."

That word was spoken in answer to an inquiry,

the inquiry of the entirely loyal but somewhat
matter-of-fact apostle St. Thomas, who said, "We
know not whither thou goest; how know we the
way?" Let us always remember that Christianity
does not offer us any detailed description of the
perfected social order for mankind. There are
symbolic pictures of the heavenly city and of the
life of heaven itself. Often those pictures are
drawn, so to speak, in musical terms, and von
Hügel used to delight to point out that when
heaven is described in terms of music it is always
a chorus or an orchestra, and never a solo. But
that is very nearly all that is to be said about it.
There is no such thing given to us as a Christian
social ideal. If there were, perhaps it might be
free from the difficulties which are aroused in most
of our minds by the social ideals drawn by men
of limited or no inspiration. But when I study
these from Plato's *Republic* onward, I am afflicted
by two difficulties. The first is that I could not
myself endure to live in the ideal society which
anyone else has sketched; and the second is that
I see no way of getting from where we are to that
place.

I remember that Plato himself hoped to accomplish the transition by banishing all citizens over
the age of ten and undertaking the education of
the remainder himself. But I have no means of
doing that in any extant country. I am reminded
of the man who went to Ireland and asked the
way to Roscommon, and was met with the question,

" Is it Roscommon you want to go to?" "Yes,
it is," he said. "Well, if I wanted to go Roscommon, I wouldn't be starting from here."

That is the difficulty about all these social ideals,
that there is provided no means of transition from
where we are to the place where we are bidden to
arrive. Christianity offers no such picture of the
goal. It is true that we know not whither He is
leading us; in answer to the question, " We know
not whither thou goest; how know we the way? "
the answer is, " I am the way." And that way
always starts from where we are. There is no
circumstance in life in which it is not possible for
us to consider what is the mind of Christ and conform our own thought and conduct to it. It is
always possible to begin behaving as a Christian,
or at least more like a true Christian than we have
done before. That is the way offered to us to
follow through the world and beyond it, but of
course such an enterprise can only be undertaken
by faith, by trust (that is), in Him who makes the
declaration that He is Himself the way.

Is this demand for faith either excessive or avoid-
able, and must we always start with an interpretation as well as a fact? I have said that it is indispensable to Christian doctrine that we should
believe both that He actually came and that it
was actually He who came. Must we start always
with an interpretation? Can we not get a naked
fact really assured and begin from there?

No, never! There is no such thing in all human

experience as a naked fact. We interpret as we perceive, from earliest infancy. The very process of receiving impressions is always interpretative; and with the interpretation there is the possibility, of course, of mistake. And so there is nothing peculiar here, though the degree of interpretation demanded no doubt is, so to speak, higher in comparison with the affirmation of fact than it is in ordinary experience of the senses; but it is nothing in principle peculiar, for there is no such thing as a mere experienced fact upon which interpretation has to be built.

Thus we start with the apostolic testimony. We start with the proclamation of the apostles concerning the Word made flesh, " the Gospel of Jesus Christ the Son of God." There the words stand at the head of the earliest of the Gospels. We know that interpretation has entered into their apprehension. But once we have learned that that is the universal principle of all apprehension, we cannot wish it otherwise.

Suppose that our Lord had written a book in which He had laid down formulated doctrine and precise directions for conduct. Then such a book would have been a fetter upon the free movement of the mind; for those who accepted His divine authority it would be final, whether their own spiritual apprehension could reach to it or not. And there would have been introduced into the heart of faith a mechanical element from which we are freed by the very fact that we know Him

ship of the Christian with his Lord does not in the smallest degree resemble the kind of communication which spiritualists believe to be possible between the spirits of the departed and ourselves. It is an intimate, personal fellowship. Of course, it is possible to regard it as a hallucination; but it is a remarkably persistent one. It arises under the most astonishing conditions, and above all it happens to men of every race and of every period. It is the familiar experience of missionaries that their converts always think of our Lord as a fellow countryman, even a fellow tribesman, of their own. All humanity finds in Him the satisfaction of the desire of its soul.

That kind of fellowship with Him would be a thing entirely incredible if He were only a human being like other human beings through whom, in special manner, the spirit of God spoke and acted. But if He is indeed Himself eternal God, in whom we live and move and have our being, then it is just what we should expect to find—that as we study that story we are in presence of and fellowship with the eternal.

And the story is the story of love gaining its sovereignty through sacrifice. From the moment when, at His baptism, He feels called upon to take His Messianic mission, He lays aside in the three temptations the only extant forms of Messianic expectation. He will not use His power to satisfy His own or other people's creature wants; He will not bribe men into the Kingdom; He will not

D

exert force and be a Cæsar-Christ, winning the kingdoms of the world by overwhelming them so that they must come in whether they will or no. He will not give irresistible evidence of His divine origin, appearing in the temple courts upborne by angels, so that doubt becomes impossible and men must accept Him whether their hearts go out to Him or not.

All the great conceptions that have existed—the Messianic banquet, the Davidic king, the apocalyptic figure coming in the clouds of heaven—all are laid aside. He goes into the world to live the life of perfect love, using the power which is His, always and only for love's sake. He chooses twelve that they may be with him, and as they begin, no doubt in a kind of awe-struck groping, to appreciate the companion with whom they are walking through the countryside, He asks them first whom men take Him to be, and then whom they themselves suppose Him to be. And St. Peter, with a leap of inspired insight, answers, " Thou art the Christ," the promised Messiah.

At once, the moment He has been freely recognized, He begins to give a new teaching that He had never given before and which He now gives repeatedly: The Son of Man must suffer. There is the great thing that He will do. There is the focus of His Messianic authority. At that same moment He starts upon the journey to Jerusalem that will end with the triumphal entry by which He challenges the authorities and precipitates the

Passion. And before the high priests He declares
that the prophecies are indeed fulfilled. "From
henceforth "—not hereafter, a most disastrous blun-
der of the translators—" there shall be the Son of
Man seated on the right hand of power "—Daniel's
prophecy here and now fulfilled, because love is
reaching its complete expression, and through that
complete expression will win its power over the
hearts of men.

I know, of course, that in giving that outline
sketch I beg many questions, but it is the reading
of the story which seems to do most justice of any
that I may frame to all the elements that are set
before us and to fit with the experience of the
Christian Church.

But one last word: If, indeed, we accept this
tremendous affirmation of the Church concerning
the Word made flesh, it must become the centre of
a whole philosophy. There we see the material—
and St. John no doubt chose the word " flesh "
because it represents the material in just that phase
most commonly associated with evil, though of
course in order to insist that such association is
not necessary—there we see the material taken
and made into the vehicle of the spiritual. There
you see the sacramental principle in its fullest
development and expression. And there you have
a clue to the understanding of the world and the
mastery of the world, that the material always
exists in order to be the expression and the vehicle
of what is spiritual, and that spirit, at least in this

world, most of all exhibits itself by using and controlling the material.

And so you have a Christian conception of the spiritual life quite different from that of Neo-Platonism or of Buddhism. The spiritual is not to be found by turning our backs upon the material and leaving it to go its own way. But the spiritual is above all to be found by facing the material in fellowship with God and using it to become the expression of the divine character as that reproduces itself in our own souls through the faith in us which it has itself evoked.

And so the Incarnation becomes the pivot of a whole philosophical system which sees the universe itself as a sacrament grounded in the love of God and ministering to the upbuilding of a society of spirits which exhibits the love which created them and returns that love. And at the same time it becomes the inspiring force or power which enables men to overcome the evil of the world until at last the kingdoms of the world become the kingdom of our God and of His Christ—" This is the victory which overcometh the world, even our faith."

CHAPTER III

SIN AND ATONEMENT

ONE of the chief difficulties in our work as ministers of the Gospel, as from another point of view it is one of the difficulties of the world at large, is that that world has so greatly lost any sense of sin, and consequently lost any sense of the need for atonement. I suppose this has partly happened because there has come to be a sharper division between those who are in any way regular worshippers and those who ignore the claims of religion, with the result that those who have let worship drop out of their lives have no standard by which to judge themselves and be convicted of sin, while those who are worshippers are for the most part such as are able to live up at least to the standard that public opinion expects of them. And in such a case, it is only through first appreciation of the holiness of God that the sense of sin can revive.

I think most of us, if we are quite honest, have to admit that our consciences depend a good deal upon the public opinion of the society in which we move; and if we are behaving in the kind of way that that society expects and doing nothing that will scandalize it, we find it difficult of ourselves to be permanently conscious of sin.

In moments of special apprehension of the divine holiness, that sense of sin is bound to revive. If a man should claim to have had a vision of God which did not bring him to penitence, I should feel very sure either that he had had no real vision, or that it was not a vision of the real God.

But when we are confronted with such a situation as we have to deal with now, it is necessary to try to think the matter out afresh, not in the expectation of finding any new truth, but in the hope of newly grasping the old truth. And we may notice that this whole subject has been approached in different periods of the Church's history along quite different lines.

Broadly speaking, Greek patristic theology is all worked out in terms of substance or nature. We know how the whole doctrine of the person of Christ was developed in those terms; and it is very difficult, while employing almost exclusively those terms, to give what we should regard as an adequate place to the ethical side of human life or of the divine claim upon us. It is noticeable that redemption in the Greek Fathers is more often spoken of as the imparting of incorruptibility to that which was corruptible, and of immortality to that which was mortal, than of holiness to that which was sinful. These were the terms in which the contrast most naturally arose. On the other hand, the Greek terms provided in an almost unique degree a vehicle for expressing that sense of personal union through Christ with the Father which it is the whole purpose of the Incarnation and Atonement to effect.

When you turn to the Latin Fathers the categories of law come to prevail, because these were the categories most familiar to citizens under the more direct influence of Rome. The great imperial system and its centre, though it had embraced the eastern Mediterranean, never supplanted there the older philosophical tradition in its influence upon men's thoughts; but in the West it was itself the dominant tradition, and consequently the terminology of law was that which was nearest at hand, and most easily conveyed to the people the truth which was to be imparted. The strong point of that approach is its manifestly ethical character. The weak point is that in terms of law it is difficult to express the spiritual union which is the consummation of faith. The Greek theories were defective on the ethical side; the Latin and scholastic theories defective on the more intimate spiritual side.

We are living in a world where the leading terms of thought are drawn from the natural sciences, and especially in this connection from biological evolution. There have been attempts made to explain what the Church calls sin in purely evolutionary terminology. We have, most of us, no doubt come across the suggestion that mankind is afflicted with this moral problem because it has inherited from the past powerful animal impulses, while the distinctively human quality of reason, or spirit, is still in process of development and has not yet won complete control. Or, again, we have seen a learned theologian, not very long ago, Dr. N. P. Williams, in his Bampton Lectures, after a quite masterly survey of the doctrine of the Fall and Original Sin as held in the past, offer the suggestion that Original Sin is, in fact, a defect of the gregarious instinct. Apparently he identifies this with moral altruism, and supposes that if we can strengthen the gregarious instinct the balance will be restored. It is a little difficult, in the face of mass movements of terrible power such as we have seen in the world of late, to make the assumption that the gregarious instinct is necessarily a source of more good than evil.

But none of these purely evolutionary theories touches the centre of the problem, for no man who is really conscious of sin will be content to have that consciousness explained as merely an indication that his growth is as yet incomplete. He knows quite well that it is something other than that. It is not simply that he sees before him a goal he has not yet reached, but that he has seen a goal before him and has turned his back upon it; and every one of us knows in his own heart that the secret of his sin is a quite definite refusal of the claim and call of God.

I think we can perhaps take some suggestion from each of the views that I have mentioned, and try to set the matter out once more in the light of at least one contemporary view of the universe, not expecting that this, any more than the others, will, of itself, give us the whole truth, but in the hope that it will set us moving along a line which enables us to commend the truth to the people of our generation.

According to this view—and I think it is almost universally held, though the phrasing would vary from one exponent to another—reality exists in a series of strata of which it is sufficient to indicate the stages of matter, life, mind, and spirit. These are related to one another in such a way that the lower is necessary to the higher, but only fulfils its own destiny when the higher comes upon it and utilizes it, or, in the old phrase, " informs " it. Thus, life is only apparent in the living material organism. But we should never have known what might be the capacities of matter unless we had seen it used as the instrument of life. Again, mind, using the word for the moment as the calculation of means to ends that are fixed, only appears as assisting the life of the organism. Both the lower stages are necessary to it, but the meaning of both those lower stages is disclosed more fully when seen under the direction of mind than they could have been before. And once more, spirit or reason, conceived as the capacity to choose between ends and not only to select means to an end already fixed, only appears where there is already a thinking, living organism. But, once again, thought and the life and organism which it controls are greatly modified by the presence of spirit exercising a still superior control. And it is at that last stage that we find, for the first time, a conscious sense of value. Not only, as seems to be the case with the animals, are some particular things recognized as desirable and others as undesirable, but there is a sense of the very principle of value itself, an understanding or knowledge of good and evil.

So soon as that happens it is at least most highly probable that the finite spirit, having a narrow range of apprehension and not having, therefore, the natural power to see things in their true perspective, will regard as more important those which affect itself, and so, in the moment when full moral self-consciousness arises, self-centredness arises with it. And self-centredness is sin.

It is not true that we are the proper centre about which all that affects us should revolve. God is the one centre of the world and of all creatures, and life can only be truly lived when it is lived in relation to God as centre, and when the finite spirits recognize themselves not only in thought but in feeling to be, as it were, planets revolving about that sun.

With this capacity for understanding good and evil as principles, and therefore of choosing between possible ends of life, as for example between duty and pleasure, there necessarily arises in its rudimentary form what we call freedom. I suggest that what we mean by freedom as applied to the human will is the capacity to do what seems to us good, and the trouble is that what seems to us good

is not at first, or by nature, what really is good.
We start, so to speak, with a handicap. It is in
our nature; it is original. And the great myth
with which the Bible opens sets the whole thing
very vividly before us. It is by attaining to knowledge of good and evil that man involves himself
also in the entanglement of sin.

Then see what is bound to happen and what we
know, as a matter of fact, does happen. Here is
the self, giving undue prominence to that which
concerns itself. And over against it are other
selves doing the same. The self-assertive and the
self-defensive impulses will increase the self-centredness, and by process of imitation the gregarious
instinct will do just the same. The finite selves,
each of them trying to be the centre of the life
it lives, are brought into a competitive relationship
with one another from the outset; and so the thing
mounts up from the individual level through the
competition or rivalries of families and tribes and
nations and races to the whole massed accumulation
of evil which is the problem of our world.

I do not think anyone can deny that, even
though there may be other things also to be said,
we are here upon the track of one root, at least, of
man's sin. It is really very extraordinary that
people should, at this time of day, not be conscious
of sin in general, or should be impatient of concern
with it. A distinguished man of science said in
England—I suppose it is now about thirty years
ago—that " the modern man is not worrying about

his sins." Perhaps the world would be a bit better if he were. The cut-throat competition and rivalries between different classes, between different nations, look as though they may be reducing the world to a shambles, and men go on saying that they see no reason to trouble about their sins. Where do they think all this comes from? The great evils of society do not result from the startling and appalling wickedness of some few individuals; they are the result of a few million people like ourselves living together; and if anyone wants to see the picture of his sin, let him look at slums, and wars, and the like. These things have their origin in characters like ours, ready, no doubt, to be generous with superfluities, but in the last resort self-centred with alike the defensiveness and aggressiveness that go with that self-centredness.

Selfhood, or being a self, is the basis both of all spiritual good and of all spiritual evil. This is the point where that facile and superficial evolutionary suggestion breaks down. The seat of sin is the very organ of our moral improvement and of our communion with God. It is in the spiritual life itself, and that is why we cannot cure it. It is a corruption in the very capacity of aspiration. In some degree the light which is in us is darkness.

Of course, that is not the whole truth. Some seek consolation in the fact that there are good tendencies in human nature from the beginning as well as bad. And if we were approaching the matter in the spirit of physicists we should just take note of the fact that men are born both good and bad, and we must deal with them accordingly. But we are approaching the matter as those who believe that the world is created by omnipotent goodness, and the problem is that there should be any evil there at all.

Sin does not mean merely being upon the wrong side of an average line; it means " falling short of the glory of God "; everything about us which falls short of the glory of God is sin, and the world cannot be free from its troubles until it is freed from sin so understood. We have, most of us, heard complaints that the language used by the Church on this subject is exaggerated and even morbid. Why should we call ourselves miserable sinners? Well, of course, if by " miserable " you mean unhappy, it may not be true. Most of us are deplorably happy sinners. But if you mean by miserable what the word really means—that is, pitiable—then we are, when viewed in the light of the divine righteousness and love, most pitiable sinners. And if anyone does not feel that the burden of his sin is intolerable, I can only once more invite him to look at slum dwellings and the threat of war.

And so man is in a state of tension from which he cannot deliver himself. I find great occasion for alarm in very much of that modern practice of psychotherapy from which no doubt we are also going to gain great benefits. But in some of this practice there is a strong suggestion that all we have to do is somehow to become at peace with ourselves, to restore an internal harmony, to become, as they like to say, fully integrated. And I want to ask, about what centre?—with what manner of self is my whole being to be harmonized?

In passing, it is perhaps one of the consolations in face of the bewildering problem of some kinds of lunacy to reflect that lunacy at least often (I do not at all suppose always) represents an internal tension between good and evil which had become unbearable. But if so, it means that the good is still struggling, and in the light of eternity there is hope. While there are some people entirely contented and sane and normal who have achieved that equilibrium because they have made peace with their own sin; and while that lasts there is for them no hope; something must break it up.

Now, if this is an account of the state of man, not complete but true so far as it goes, what is it that he needs? Nothing less than to be reconstructed about God as centre of his being, so that he comes to see himself as one, and only one, in the family of God, and this not by compulsion, so that there is an element in him which still resists, but by winning him freely to accept that status.

The man cannot so reconstruct himself. Why not? Why, because he doesn't want to. That, of course, is always the problem. As St. Augustine pointed out, I will to move my hand, and it moves. If there is no physical lesion or other impediment, the motion is the immediate expression of the volition. You don't have to think how to do it. I will to move my will, and it does not move. Why not? Why, because if my will to move it were whole-hearted it would be unnecessary, for it would have moved already. The fact that you have at all to will that your will should be better than it is, shows that the instrument of your action is itself corrupted. Something must take hold of you from without. You can't do it for yourself. All you can do, and that is possible, is, in moments when the better purpose is uppermost, to submit yourself to the influences which have the transforming power. As a matter of wisdom in the handling of souls I cannot help thinking we have attended too much to the bad moments which have issued in sinful acts, and have not usually sufficiently urged people to make the most of their best times, because those are the times when there is hope; and if, whenever aspiration becomes strong, we would always turn our attention in that direction from which sanctifying power comes, our progress would be more rapid. But the transformation must be effective not against, but through, our exercise of freedom. Otherwise it cannot be complete, but will leave us still in the state of tension with some part of our nature still rebellious.

Is there, in fact, anything known in the world which does control conduct by means of and not by over-riding freedom? Yes; one thing only —the sacrifice of love.

When a man finds that someone else has such love for him that he has been willing to suffer for that love, there is hardly anyone so hard as to remain indifferent. I do not say that such knowledge will always and at once overcome all selfishness in that regard, but it will be a strong pull. We know that there is no action in life in which we feel so free as an action that we undertake in order to please a friend; yet the content of that action, the thing we do, is then determined by the pleasure of our friend; it is, so to speak, he who has really chosen what shall be done, and yet there is nothing that we do so freely. It is in the mutual interaction of love that there is to be found the power which does control the will through and not against its freedom.

With such thoughts in mind we turn to the Gospel and the Church's doctrine. We have heard it said over and over again that the promise of the Gospel is that we shall be forgiven if we repent. I should like to point out in passing that our Lord never said that. If we mean the whole truth of the word by repentance, then the saying is true. But it is not what He said, and there is something else which He said which puts that truth in its most searching form. What He said was, " You shall be forgiven if you forgive." And at once you see it makes all the difference in the world whether you come to God saying, " I am truly sorry and I mean never to do it again," or whether you come to God saying, " I am truly sorry, but I have forgiven everyone who has injured me," because in the one case you come as an isolated individual, almost making a claim upon God because you have fulfilled His condition; in the other you come as one member of His family, knowing that you have no claim except what His love grants to all.

Repentance means a change of heart and the acceptance of God's view of the world instead of our own. St. Peter was once called Satan on the ground that he thought like a man instead of thinking like God. And of course, if we could accept the divine standpoint, if our mind were the mind of Christ, then we should always be forgiving. Therefore it is true that if we repent and mean the whole of what the word ought to mean, we are in the state to receive the divine forgiveness. But however we understand it, the trouble is, how are we to repent?

Coleridge said, on one occasion, I think with great truth, that the supreme promise of the Gospel is not forgiveness to those who repent, but repentance to those who sin. It is no use telling me that I shall be forgiven if I repent when I don't repent, unless you go on to tell me how to do it. But if our Lord is what we believe Him to be, then the picture of the love of God presented in the Cross, representing what our self-centredness is meaning to Him, must begin to draw us out of that self-centredness. We cannot any longer think that what matters to us is more important than what

E

matters to others, when our taking that view means all this to Him. There you get your new standard of value presented in such a way as appeals not only to the mind, but to the heart, which matters more.

Moreover, by the Cross God makes His own act of forgiveness righteous. You are familiar with the Hindu objection to the Christian doctrine, that it is immoral because it teaches forgiveness of sin, whereas the Hindu doctrine of Karma is strictly just, for it insists that upon every soul there is visited the precise equivalent of its conduct. And that would be true if the divine forgiveness were expressed in the form, "Never mind; we won't think about it any more."

No man of sensitive conscience could be willing to accept forgiveness on such terms. It would be insulting. There is nothing so insulting to a man as to pretend that his moral lapses do not matter. It is to treat him as below the moral level. And if we have reached that level at all, then nothing could be more dreadful for us than to suppose that God said, "Never mind." There is only one thing worse, I have heard it said, than to break your mother's heart, and that is to find out that she had no heart to be broken.

But the Christian who has heard his word of pardon from the lips of Christ upon the Cross is never in danger of supposing that God does not mind. He minds, like that. And so, as St. Paul says, Christ as set forth upon the Cross shows the righteousness of God in the very act of forgiveness. This is part—I know not whether it be the whole, but this is part—at least of that which Christian tradition has stood for in its insistence that the mere appeal of love to our souls is not sufficient as an account of the Atonement—that there must also be in a true sense a propitiation toward God. This divine act has been wrought. The power is there in the world. From the moment of the Passion the Son of Man is coming with the clouds of heaven. The coming is permanent: "Behold, He cometh with the clouds." But the full apprehension of it, and consequently the full effect of it, is future: "Every eye shall see Him."

How do we make the fruit of that act our own? By faith. But what does faith mean here? Faith always, of course, includes an element of belief, if that is the word for the intellectual acceptance. But it is always something very much more than belief: it is practical and personal trust; and when you trust in somebody with completeness the result is that his will begins to direct your own, again freely, because your trust must be freely given or else it is not trust at all. But if his will directs your own, then, in a very real moral sense, you are incorporated into his personality or, as the New Testament would say, into His body. And as we trust in the love of God, directing the eyes of heart and mind towards the picture of it that He has given, it may take possession of our souls, and what seems out of tune with it will become repellent to us, so that what we had once liked we like no longer, and what we had once shrunk from becomes attractive.

We are no longer, then, in the position of those who receive their orders and have to obey them for fear of punishment or in hope of reward, which is the state of bondage, the status of the slave. But we have not received the spirit of slavery again, that we should fear, but the spirit of adoption. The love of God made manifest in righteousness draws us towards itself in such a way that in the very act it cleanses us from all things unfit for that presence, and we are able to say, " Between our sins and their reward We set the passion of Thy Son our Lord," because we are also able to say, " Look, Father, look on His anointed face, And only look on us as found in Him "—that is, as we shall be—are now, please God, beginning to be —through the constraining influence of His love upon our hearts. Our duty is not primarily to strive and to brace up our wills, but primarily to fasten our attention upon the divine love, that it may do its own work upon us and within us.

Thus it is that God, by the sacrifice of His own love, has put forth the power which is able to control us through the freedom of our wills and not against it, and in doing this, to reconstruct our lives about that same divine love as centre. And the heart of moral improvement, the heart of moral progress, therefore also of social progress, and the amelioration of this world's bitter condition, is always to be found in worship, worship which is the opening of the heart to the love of God and the exposure of the conscience to be quickened by it.

These are the things that worship means: the giving of ourselves whole and entire to Him who alone has claim to such an offering. And it is because that is the nature of worship that to offer it to anything other than the true God is the deadliest of sins.

But, when all is said and done, the centre of our hope is not our reflection upon the fact, but the fact itself. Here supremely we see how true it is that a fact may be a bond of unity when theories and doctrines are liable to become sources of division. There have been many doctrines of the Atonement in the history of the Church, and some of them, at least, are incompatible with one another as intellectual formulations. But the adherents of every one of those doctrines would find themselves perfectly united as they knelt at the foot of the Cross. In the moment of adoration, directed not towards some figure of our own conceiving, drawn to represent the theories that we had fashioned, but directed towards what God Himself has done as manifestation of what eternally He is, we find at once the power over our own individual souls, and the bond of union between all others whose hearts are turned that way.

And here, too, we find part of the answer to some of the worst problems that afflict the mind of our time. I will put it in the form of a little dialogue which I quote from memory of a book that had much vogue some twenty-five years ago, *Christus Futurus*:

" ' There cannot be a God of love,' men say, ' because if there were, and He looked upon this world, His heart would break.'

" The Church points to the Cross and says, ' His heart does break.'

" ' It is God who has made the world,' men say, ' it is He who is responsible, and it is He who should bear the load.'

" The Church points to the Cross and says, ' He does bear it.'

" ' God is beyond men's comprehension, and it is blasphemy to say you know Him; ' and the Church answers, ' We do not know Him perfectly; but we worship the majesty we see.' "

CHAPTER IV

CHRISTIANITY, ETHICS AND POLITICS

THE subject of this lecture is on a different plane from those which have preceded it. I was a little doubtful about adding a discussion of this kind of question to that series, but was told that there was some special interest in it, and of course all that I can do is to outline the method which seems to me most appropriate for the Christian approach to ethical and political problems.

I am not now concerned, specially, with the construction of an ideal system of Christian ethics. No one doubts the close connection between Christianity and ethics, understanding by the term " ethics " a system of principles or directions by which conduct ought to be regulated. But the actual problems of ethical and political life mainly concern not pure ethics, but applied ethics. And the application is nearly always to a situation in which the ideal has been already to some extent frustrated, and in face of such a situation it is nearly always true that there is no course possible which is not open to serious objection.

There is a real entanglement of sin, and once evil has entered into human relationships there is, as a rule, no method of dealing with it against which very serious criticism cannot be brought. Perhaps part of the trouble is due to the fact that we who have to take action in relation to a situation infected with evil are infected with it also ourselves. If we were perfect Christian saints we could take courses of action which at present are either out of our reach or would be inappropriate for persons of our character, because they would so easily raise a charge of hypocrisy.

Our first necessity is to distinguish the meanings of certain questions that are often asked. For example, there is the question, What ought the Church to do with regard to the marriage problem, the unemployment problem, the problem of peace and war? And the first thing that is necessary is to find out what the questioner means when he asks, " What is the Church to do? " Usually he has not thought about it, but is only demanding that somebody should do something.

But the question ought to mean, " What action shall be taken by the entire fellowship of Christian people acting corporately? " Or, to come as near to that as we can in practice, " What action should be taken by the official councils or assemblies of the Church? "

Usually the questioner does not mean that. Usually what he has in mind is some action to be taken by the officials and spokesmen of the Church. And then it is at once apparent that some things are only appropriate if they have already been endorsed by the official councils and assemblies.

There are things which I might find myself at liberty to say in England if the Convocation of which I am the president had already agreed upon them, which it would seem to me highly inexpedient that I should say, even if I think them, while they are still matter of debate within the Church itself.

On the other hand, there are some things which may appropriately and rightly be said by those who have the responsibility of interpreting and applying the Gospel in Christian life as a contribution to the public thought upon the matter, but which it would not be at all appropriate to submit for endorsement to any official Christian assembly.

There is the further question, or possible meaning of the first question, " What are Christian people to do in their social and civic capacity? " And all of these are quite different, and the people who ask the question, especially when making a demand that the Church should act, have usually jumbled them all together in their mind. I find that it causes, as a rule, very profound irritation when some eager agitator is asked which of these various meanings he desires to have attached to his question.

Now, to me it seems clear that what our Lord has done for us is to lay down certain principles for application which are themselves expressive of a spirit in which we are to live, but that He always leaves to us the question how those principles are in fact to be applied. And I propose to discuss for a few moments the extraordinarily difficult question of the attitude, both of the Church officially and of Christian people individually, to marriage and the complications that may arise concerning it, precisely because this is just now so controversial and because we are all of us engaged in trying to think out more clearly what our line of conduct should be. I think it highly probable that no one will agree with all the things I say, and that those who most agree with some will be most passionate in their disagreement with others.

There is no doubt about the Christian principle of marriage in general. It is the principle of lifelong union of one man with one woman to the exclusion of all others.

I think that if you take the various passages in the New Testament which deal with marriage and the relation of the sexes, you will find that the one principle which finds expression in them all is that physical union can only be right when it is accompanied by and is the expression of a personal union so close that of its nature it must be lifelong, and that anything less than that is always short of the ideal.

It is, for example, a quite necessary inference, as I think, from the language of St. Paul upon that subject, that sexual irregularity before marriage makes true marriage forever impossible. And if that is the necessary deduction from his language, then, of course, we have to notice that the Church has never felt able to apply that standard in practice. That is rather important in view of the subsequent questions that must arise concerning its action when other departures from the ideal have taken place.

When we turn to our Lord's own teaching, there are two points to which I want to call attention. The first is what I have already said, that the only true principle is that of strict and absolute monogamy. But the second is that Moses is quite certainly not censured for having made a concession to the hardness of men's hearts. The censure is for the hard-hearted men, and not for Moses, who had to take some steps for dealing with a situation where men had already departed from the ideal.

Then let us notice that the functions of the Church and of the State in connection with such a matter are quite different. It is probably more necessary to dwell upon this in my own country than in yours, for in England until not very long ago the State's law of marriage was avowedly based upon the Church's law, and to this moment the only possible ground for divorce is adultery, real or presumed. Now, the business of the Church, acting as the whole united Christian fellowship, is always to bear its witness with the utmost clarity to the true ideal. It is not primarily concerned in its handling of such a question with any inquiry about what may at the moment be practicable. Probably in administration it will have to attend to that; but it comes to that quite consciously as a descent to lower ground, and its primary business is witness to the Christian principle.

The State, on the other hand, is always primarily concerned with making the best that can be made out of the material to hand in a period which falls within reasonable calculation, and this may be something far less than the ideal.

Moreover, the Gospel seeks to carry us by its appeal to a level which is demonstrably unattainable by means of coercion. The action of the State, though it goes far beyond coercion, always in the last resort rests upon coercion for its effectiveness. Consequently we have to think at all times how far an ideal towards which we would have men aspire can truly be served by any element of coercion. And I should like to say, dogmatically, that I think the greatest delusion into which men can fall in this department of thought is that of supposing that the State will better do its duty to God if it treats every sin as a crime. What it has always to consider is whether its methods are capable of producing the kind of virtue which is aimed at.

If I may take an illustration from your own recent experience, I should not have the impertinence to pronounce any opinion in public on the question whether your experiment of prohibition can have been justified. But I will say this, that if it was justified, it must have been not because drunkenness is wicked, but because at that time drunkenness was so specially disastrous to social welfare. With wickedness as such the State has simply nothing to do. And if the State begins to base its penal action upon moral assessments, it finds itself involved in usurping the prerogatives of God and attempting to pronounce judgment where no man has the necessary knowledge.

It can deal with the social effects of any action of an individual or of a class of persons. These can be assessed by men. But the question of moral praise or blame is so far beyond the possibility of our assessment that we dare not base public action, backed by coercive power, upon what may be so erroneous an estimate.

The State, then, will make its laws, having regard to the best social welfare which it seems likely that it can promote by the means at the State's disposal. And the Christian citizen, acting politically, having his own Christian standard of what social welfare is, will use his influence to promote that welfare in ways in which the State can assist, and also to hold the State off from action which, however well intended, would have the actual effect of damaging rather than assisting the cause.

But the Church, all the more because here the State is taking care of the immediately practicable, should find some way, at least, of bearing a quite unambiguous witness to the ideal with which it is entrusted, and for that reason, as it seems to me, the Church should decline ever to sanction the use of its own Marriage Service in the case of any person who has a partner to a former marriage still living, and this should, in my judgment, be applied quite equally to the so-called innocent and the so-called guilty party, partly because of the impossibility of truly assessing moral guilt in the matter.

Of course, with a marriage law like ours, where there must be either real or presumed adultery before divorce takes place, the Church is quite at liberty to say to the man (for it is always the man when this is done) who stages, so to speak, a sham offence, that if he is not guilty of adultery he is guilty of perjury, and that from the Church's point of view it makes very little difference. He has taken up the position of the guilty party, and must accept the consequences.

That seems to me perfectly fair; but merely to stand upon that in drawing the kind of distinction which would be involved if the Church were always ready to remarry the innocent party would, in fact, I think very much obscure, in the world where we live and where people know that so often the real guilt is not the presumed guilt, our witness to the true principle.

What are we to say about the occasional and undoubted hard cases, some of them most grievously hard? Here it would seem to me that the Church must still give its witness to the true ideal principle. But I should not find myself at liberty to say, dogmatically and universally, to everyone whose first marriage has been unhappy, that under no conceivable circumstances can it now be right that he or she should contract another so long as the former partner lives. I should feel bound to throw all my general advice that way. But if a person that

I knew to be a sincere Christian should say to me, " I know, of course, that this is not ideal; I know that my former marriage was a mistake, but it was that one which was the mistake; it was then that we were joined together not by God and I believe that I am now right in the sight of God in marrying this other partner where I feel quite sure of my ground," I should say, " The Church cannot approve that; but this is not necessarily to condemn it." If the Church has done its utmost to confront the individual conscience with the *prima facie* claim of the true principle, I do not think it can then rightly pronounce judgment upon the action of that conscience afterwards.

I do not quite know why we tend to act differently in this case from the way in which we act in other moral issues. There is always a *prima facie* obligation to tell the truth. But there are some circumstances in which we recognize that it is not only permissible, but obligatory, to say what is false. The stock instance, of course, is that of the murderer asking which way his victim has gone. Stock instances are always extreme ones for the sake of clearness. We are all familiar with instances arising perpetually in daily life where to tell the truth would be monstrous, where concealment or silence is the right policy if it is possible, but where at least a suggestion of falsehood is better, morally better, than the release, let us say, of some secret which it is really important to vital issues to conceal.

I know all this is very dangerous; but I am

also quite sure that the only way to overcome the dangers of this situation is to admit them and face them; to pretend that any general moral rule is of quite universal application is a way of shirking the problem and not facing it. " Thou shalt not kill " had to be converted into " Thou shalt do no murder " before it could be universal. And that is universal, because murder is such killing as is wrong.

And so there must be an area left here, also, to the free play of the individual conscience, though it is the Church's obligation to see that the matter is presented to conscience, and is not determined on the basis of whim.

But, then, when an irregularity that it is impossible to condone takes place, how are ordinary Christians to behave? As usual, by attempting to strike the fair balance between rigorism and laxity; I do not think any universal rule can be given; the circumstances in which it can be right for a Christian to withhold friendship on account of some moral lapse must be very few, for to do that will, in most cases, mean letting someone who most needs moral help be left to the society of people unable to provide it. If we have any responsibility for one another's spiritual welfare we cannot, as a rule, meet that responsibility by methods of ostracism. There may be some cases where action of that kind will be effective in stimulating conscience for the first time. There will be far more where such action will have the effect of merely making the offending person resolute in his resistance to moral claims. You will merely put his back up.

On the other hand, if you do not resort to that, you are responsible for seeing that you do not give the impression either to the parties concerned or to the community generally that you regard the bad conduct as trifling; what is asked of us, as I think, is something very much more difficult either than merely to continue friendship or merely to abandon it, and that is to do that thing of which St. Paul speaks quite casually, as if it were nothing, showing what a saint he was, and which most of us find nearly impossible, to " speak the truth in love."

It costs a good deal to explain to someone that one has disapproved his conduct though one is still ready to be of any service to him that one can, and it is peculiarly difficult to do that in such a way as not to seem, and even to be, a prig. But a Christian has over and over again to take the risk of seeming priggish and to protect himself from actually becoming so by the discipline of his own life, which keeps him morally humble.

Then, once more, there is the question of the Church's pastoral care of those who have been at some stage guilty of irregularity. This mainly devolves upon the responsible officers of the Church, and particularly the bishops. The kind of problem presented to one may be illustrated in this way: Here is a man who has undoubtedly broken off a former marriage through infidelity. The woman

F

he has married is now—perhaps was at the time—
a good woman, spiritually minded. She has influenced her husband; children have been born
and are growing up. The time comes for their
Confirmation. Are their parents to be allowed to
accompany them to Holy Communion? Can it be
right that in such circumstances, when there seems
to be a real desire to be going on the right way,
for the sake of upholding a general principle you
should say that those children are to be exposed
to the tremendous pressure of temptation involved
in a situation where they are bidden to be regular
in their Communions and the parents are prohibited
from coming?

Personally, I have never felt able, in such a case
as I have described—I have deliberately made it
as strong as I could—to take that line. I know
there are some who say one ought—who say sharply,
" The two people are living in sin. There is an
end of it." But we are all living in sin. " Oh, yes,"
you say; " but the difference is that other people
are presumed to be penitent; and you cannot
presume penitence here because that must be
expressed by their separation." I say that their
separation at this stage would be merely another
sin, and it cannot be right to demand as the condition of restoration after a past sin that people
should now sin against their new love and against
their children.

There are at least three points to be considered:
(1) the permanent maintenance of the true principle;

(2) the pastoral care of the individuals chiefly concerned, which may include the assertion of the true principle against their wishes as well as the assistance of their progress in Christian living; (3) the witness before the contemporary community alike to the permanent principle and to the spirit of charity in its application.

Well, I have stated those positions as I hold them, not because I attach very great importance to my judgment on this matter, for any one man can see only part of the way round the problem, but because it seems to me very important that we should be trying to think about this, as about other matters, realistically. And as soon as we do this, it illustrates with particular vividness the kind of method that I think must be adopted as the Christian approaches any problem of applied ethics. He knows what his ideal is; he must find some way of bearing witness to it by speech or action or both. But then he has also got to take the tangled and vitiated situation and try to do the best he can with it. And if he is successful in finding a way of doing something that really helps the parties concerned, while he also bears his witness to the principle, he has probably got as near to the right line of action in that instance as he can come.

I turn from the more definitely ethical to the more political type of problem. Here also we must recognize that Church and State have different functions, and that the member of the Church is

also a citizen. He has his duty in each capacity.
And the indications of those two obligations may
not be the same. He will be, therefore, very for-
tunate if he can find ways of discharging both
through appropriate channels. But at least we
have to recognize that here, as always, the State
is concerned with the question, what is the best
thing that is practicable within a reasonable period,
whereas the Church is entrusted with proclaiming
a Gospel by which neither the preacher himself
nor any of his hearers are going to live perfectly
to the end of their days:

> "Lo, from afar I summon you anigh Him;
> Lo, to the multitudes I call and say,
> 'This is my King.' I preach and I deny Him,
> Christ whom I crucify afresh to-day."

At least we have to bear our testimony so far
as we can, however little consistent with our lives
it may be. " Practise what you preach " is admirable advice as an ideal counsel, but if it were
possible for the preacher to follow it out, it would
show that he was preaching very badly.

But besides this fact that the State is concerned
with the best to be made of existing material in the
next few generations, there is also to be remembered
the fact that in the application of principles to
actual situations questions of judgment arise concerning which equally loyal Christians rightly
differ. The Gospel does not give us any help
in determining what political methods are likely
to lead to the result we want in any given situation,

and you may have two groups of people perfectly united about their ultimate goal who differ diametrically about the way that will be most effective in reaching it. And therefore the Church, as a corporate society, should, as I think, never espouse a policy, because there can be no policy which does not contain such questions of judgment.

On the other hand, the Church as a society must, through its appropriate channels, which will chiefly mean its officers, announce the principles that should guide Christian people in their efforts to form policy or to choose between the policies presented to them. It should go beyond that: it should point out that there are features—for there always have been, are, and I suppose always will be—in the social life of the community concerned which constitute repudiation, or at least very inadequate expression, of fundamental Christian principles.

Take such a situation as arises around places where great masses of casual labour are employed, but where the number employed from day to day is necessarily fluctuating. This is often the case in ports, for sometimes two or three ships will have come in together to be unloaded, and sometimes there is no ship still to be unloaded and none that has come in that day. You picture the scene at the dock gate, where the men are fighting one another for the opportunity to work. You ask whether such a situation can possibly be tolerated in a society which professes to believe in the Christian conception of all men as fellow children in the family of God. What to do to remedy it is another question; but it is reasonable enough that we should clamour for its remedy, and meanwhile, at least, for some mitigation of that evil. I will come back in a moment to the question what some of the great social principles of the Gospel are; but there really is possible a quite clear distinction between the forming of a policy which can be pressed upon a government and the proclamation of principles for the formation of that public opinion to which, in the end, the government must be responsive. And the second is our function.

In relation to this work the principle of vocation will apply as elsewhere. There will be some people to whom there comes the special vocation, for example, to bear witness against the un-Christian character of war and the situations that give rise to war by dedicating themselves to complete pacifism. That some people have that vocation I have no doubt whatever; and, similarly, there will be people whose vocation is steadily to point to a pure ideal of social relationships in fellowship and love, which probably cannot be translated immediately into any political programme or picture at all. It was the vocation of St. Francis to embrace holy poverty. It was the vocation of Pope Innocent III to recognize him and approve his order. But if Pope Innocent III had himself joined the Franciscans it would have been a stark dereliction of duty.

Do let us be quite clear that different people have different contributions to make in these matters and once more respect one another's consciences. Let us not condemn as a crank or a freak everybody who does something that from the contemporary standpoint seems very peculiar. Nothing was ever more peculiar than the behaviour of St. Francis. But let not those who adopt that line of action presume to say that it is the duty of everybody else to do the same. For the most part, Christian people must be engaged in action as Christian citizens; that is to say, using political machinery with a view to bringing about the best results that can be wrought by that machinery, while at the same time, through their membership in the Christian society, they are affirming the principles in their purity.

That the Church has obligations in relation to political and social matters seems to me quite indisputable. Consider, for example, what is meant —many of you know it intimately—by bad housing and overcrowding, and the immense obstacle which this places in the way of the development of the best type of moral character. By miracles of grace, even in the worst housing conditions some beautiful lives are led; but we know quite well that most slum-dwellers very largely succumb to their conditions morally. It is especially hard for the children who grow up in those conditions; to know that there are stumbling-blocks in the way of Christ's little ones and to leave them there is not very

different from putting them there; and we know
what He had to say about that.

Again, there can be no doubt that the whole
economic order is one of the greatest moral influences
upon the character of those who grow up under it.
It was not some Socialist fanatic, but that prince
of orthodox economists of the later nineteenth
century, Marshall, who said that the two strongest
influences in forming the moral character of citizens
are the religious beliefs in which they are trained
and the economic system in which they grow up.
We understand the first. The reason for the
second, of course, is that a social order or constitution of necessity represents the scale of values
that has been accepted by those people from the
interaction of whose lives it has sprung. If you
want to see it all worked out fully, look at the eighth
and ninth books of Plato's *Republic*. If men set a
very high value among objects of ambition upon
material wealth and financial power, the social
structure will come to represent that fact. Children
who are born into that society will have the constant
suggestion pressed upon them, not by anyone in
particular but by the whole life which they share,
that these are things of supreme value to men;
and they are not. It is a false and pernicious
suggestion. We must be concerned with the moral
principles that are implied in the very structure of
the society in which we live.

One of the great principles that should govern
that structure, for example, is that power should

never be divorced from social function or from responsibility for the performance of it. I suppose it is on the whole true that the society which grew up in the earlier Middle Ages, in spite of its callous crudities in many respects, was in principle more influenced by Christian ideas than any which has succeeded it. And certainly its fundamental principle was that which I have expressed, that power must always go with function and that no one ought to be allowed to exercise power or enjoy privilege except in return for and recognition of service rendered.

You think of unemployment. It is quite impossible that a Church which has among the best-known of all its scriptures a chapter that ends with the exaltation of charity above faith, and certainly concerns itself very deeply about faith, should say that it has no obligation in respect of what causes so vast a mass of human misery as unemployment; and when it turns its attention that way it finds at once that it has some principles which give very definite guidance with regard to work among and for the unemployed.

I don't think I ever appreciated, until I looked into this question in England, how deeply penetrating are our Lord's words that it is more blessed to give than to receive. So long as the work undertaken consists of doing things for the unemployed it is quite unredemptive and leads to no restoration of character. The only experiments, now I am glad to say very numerous in England and rapidly spreading, which show that effect upon character, are those which invite the unemployed to give what they can for the community. For there is one thing that they have to give in some abundance; it is that labour or power which the ordinary industrial system has not hired.

And so, to take the most signally successful of these schemes, really astonishing results in the reclamation of character have been achieved through a co-operative scheme where some who can, give a little money, and some who can, give material, and the unemployed themselves give their labour and their time, and contribute through this for the benefit of the whole community something of value which would not otherwise have been produced, such as, for example, the laying out of waste land as a park or public pleasure-ground, or the provision of a large swimming-pool; I could go on with lists of benefits conferred upon towns by the unemployed acting in co-operation with others, nobody being paid but all giving and then co-operating. The unemployed have no money to give, but they have themselves to give.

Finally, I should like to indicate what seem to me the most evident of the social principles of Christianity which we must, I think, take opportunity often to proclaim, and which we should be applying at least in the sense of showing how far our present society often is from giving effect to them. That is quite different as an application, as you perceive, from dictating a policy which says how the effect is to be given. It constitutes the public demand upon those who have the specialist knowledge that they shall find the way. First and foremost are the two great principles of the divine Fatherhood and man's eternal destiny, because these two assure to the individual a status and a dignity which are prior to his membership of any earthly state, so that the State must always treat him as someone who has a value other than his value to itself.

That is expressly denied by Communism, especially in its Russian form, and it is implicitly denied by the present systems in vogue in Italy and in Germany. We are in grave danger of a development of such State control of all which should be the spiritual concern of the individual as involves a belief that the value of the individual is only to his earthly State; and I am convinced that the only kind of freedom which either can or ought to stand against these modern pressures is the freedom which reposes upon the claim inherent in the divine Son-ship of every human being.

But beyond those two great principles which affect the relation of the State to its citizens in general there are at least four principles of universal application, which, because their application is universal, are applicable and demand application to social matters. First is this principle of freedom itself, or, to put it more strictly, the sacredness of human personality—the duty, in the Kantian phrase, always to treat human beings as ends, and never only as means. When we look at the industrial system that we have allowed to grow up it is surely quite apparent that at least in many parts of the world labourers are treated by the system, even if not so in the intention of those who work it, as only part of the means of production. And it can never be right to treat human beings so.

But the sacredness of personality might work out as a kind of egoism all round if it were not at once balanced by the other great principle of fellow-membership, that we belong to one another, a relationship only fully realized, no doubt, as all other human things are only fully realized, in the fellowship of Christ, but which is none the less a fundamental truth of human nature as God created it.

And here we may perhaps usefully reflect upon the fact that in its own nature the whole of our social order is really a fellowship, though we constantly treat it as if it were not. Reformers sometimes demand that industry should become co-operation for public service instead of competition for private profit. That puts it wrong. Industry always is co-operation for public service, but we often treat it as if it were competition for private profit. It is co-operation for private service because it can only go on so long as the various factors co-operate. Capital, management, labour—however you organize them, they must all be there; if one of them withdraws its co-operation the process stops. And it is for public service, because if no one wants the goods there will be no purchase money, and again the process cannot go on at all. In order to exist it must be co-operation for public service.

That, then, is its essence; and if we will treat something of which that is the essence as if it were competition for private profit, of course it will go wrong, because we are making a mistake.

Personality; fellowship. I will only allude to two others. The duty of service arises out of those two. If you put them together you can't escape it. In every relationship in life in which we find ourselves our duty is to be asking, what is the service I can render through the opportunities afforded by this position? Can it be said that most of our business is conducted by that principle? A great deal, yes; there is a spirit of service both toward the community and toward workpeople. Among workpeople themselves there is also often a great spirit of service, both to the firm or company and to the community, and above all to their fellow-workers. There is a great deal; but it isn't the dominant note in industry.

Yet there can be no doubt that the Christian's duty in every situation of life is to ask how, here, can I render service. And that leads on to a fourth and conspicuously Christian principle—the power of sacrifice. I am quite sure that a reading of English history—I have not tested this elsewhere—through the nineteenth century leads to this result: No social progress has been accomplished through action on the part of labour making itself a nuisance. Where strikes have been successful in achieving a measure of progress, it has been because the sacrifice endured has called vivid attention to a real grievance and has stirred the conscience of the whole community; where real progress has come, it has always been because there has been a new moral awakening, caused, not only by the trouble which the strikers have inflicted on their neighbours, but by the courage with which they have endured privation for the sake of what seemed to them a just cause.

Put that on the one side, and on the other side that it may be—none of us can ever say when this is so for another—the duty of those who have opportunities of amassing wealth to forgo those opportunities and even perhaps to face actual loss amounting to ruin in business for the sake of adherence to principle and witness to it. This would not always be right, because it must involve great suffering for many of the adherents and not only for the individual so acting; but, where such a step could rightly be taken, the witness of it would be more effective than any amount of preaching in winning recognition for the principle concerned.

Well, these, then, are some of the principles which we should urge, as I think, that all our folk and we ourselves should constantly have in mind in face of social and industrial evils. We cannot claim that those evils are no concern of ourselves, because they touch character, and character is our field. It is no business of ours to say precisely how they can be remedied; but it is the business of the Church to say that whatever departs from these principles is so far an evil that it must be cured by a fuller application of these principles, and that those who have the requisite knowledge and experience are called upon in the name of Christ to use their opportunity as Christians in the position where they are placed to that end.

PRINTED IN GREAT BRITAIN BY RICHARD CLAY & SONS, LIMITED,
BUNGAY, SUFFOLK.

GOLDEN PRESS
LIBRARY
NEW YORK